Candlewicking and Beyond

Embroidery Designs by Gary Clarke

Candlewicking
and
Beyond
Embroidery Designs

Original Embroidery Designs by Gary Clarke

THIS BOOK
BELONGS TO

....

....

Candlewicking and Beyond
is dedicated to a very gifted friend
Jill Fish

Contents

Acknowledgements

Firstly I would like to thank God
for the gifts He has given. My wife Helen and
our children Amelia and Simon.
To Madeira Australia for their product
assistance.

Finishing touches	Jill Fish
Editing	Catriona Hall
Photography	Philip Kuruvita
Printing	Altshul Printers Pty Ltd

Embroidery, Designs and Illustrations
by Gary Clarke.

ISBN   0646 30917X

Published by:

25 Izett Street Prahran Victoria 3181 Australia
Tel: 613 9529 4400 Fax: 613 9525 1172

Email: penguin@netspace.net.au
Website: http://www.penguin-threads.com.au

Candlewicking and Beyond by Gary Clarke
Printed by Altshul Printers
239 Separation Street Northcote Victoria 3070 Australia

Dear Embroiderer

I trust you will enjoy Candlewicking and Beyond. I have certainly enjoyed producing it.

Although many people use pearl thread for candlewicking and whitework, I find its pristine look unsatisfying.

Now Madeira Australia sell this beautiful, soft, 100% Australian cotton thread, which inspired me to produce this book.

The thread is very versatile, it led me from candlewicking and beyond to tassels, needle lace, crocheting and canvas work.

As always my designs are predominantly floral, a mixture of petite to bold motifs. I am sure you will find many applications for the hearts, garlands and borders, adding your own style and character.

Regards
Gary

Introduction

Candlewicking

Simplicity is the key to candlewicking, simplicity of colour, simplicity of stitch, simplicity of thread.

History suggests that candlewicking in its purest form was born of a desire to create, to decorate, where there were few resources to spend on such luxuries. The early materials were simple every day items, the thread used for candle making and recycled calico from flour sacks etc. Candlewicking enriched an otherwise austere existence.

Today we enjoy candlewicking for its simplicity, as it lends itself to the most humble of items.

The basic knot used in candlewicking is the colonial knot, although the french knot may be used. The colonial knot has the advantage of sitting more neatly on the surface of the fabric. Other simple stitches can be added for contrast.

Candlewicking for Children

Whilst demonstrating at various Stitching Shows around Australia, I find that children love to run their fingers over the knots, therefore, it is a great medium to decorate children's manchester and clothing.

The coloured thread also lends itself to "baby" or "infant" clothing and blankets, as it is soft and washes beautifully.

Beyond Candlewicking

If you like candlewicking, but would like more challenge, Candlewicking thread can adapt itself nicely to other forms of white work. Whitework encompasses white on white needlework ranging from very simple to more complex and elegant pieces.

Often the complexity of a design does not mean a greater degree of difficulty, as the stitches are still basic.

Tassels

Candlewicking thread is ideal for making tassels. I have given the technique for making a basic tassel, and several methods to create variations. These tassels are a great way to add that touch of opulence.

Introduction

Requirements

- Candlewicking cotton.
- Madeira stranded cotton.
- Size 1 milliners needle.
- Heat transfer pencil (blue.)
- Fine point, water erasable pen.
- Homespun fabric.
- Waffle weave blanketing.
- Felt (synthetic.)
- 14inch plastic canvas.

Threads

Candlewicking thread is a soft (2 ply) thread, 100% Australian cotton. The fine ply of this thread enables one to use it for fine work, whilst still having the option to double or quadruple it for heavier work. Being pure cotton this thread washes and wears well, its slightly fluffy texture will bind stitches when washed enhancing close stitches such as satin stitch.

Needle

For stitches such as bullion, french knots, colonial knot, a straw or Milliners needle are essential. I have used a size I Milliners needle for all the designs in this book, both intricate and bold.

Fabric

Although any fabric might be used for these designs, I would suggest natural cottons and linens. Many of the worked pieces have been worked on pre-shrunk home spun. Some of the padded work has been stitched onto waffle weave blanketing.

Plastic canvas

Used primarily for canvas work, and coming in many counts this canvas can also be used as a graph.

Using the canvas and a fine tipped water erasable pen, plot your design onto the fabric.

Remove the canvas and work the design either in knots or stitches.

 * (14inch count canvas used in all designs)

Transfer pencils and pens

Blue leaded heat transfer pencil

Trace your chosen design onto grease proof paper using the pencil. Place the paper face down onto the fabric and iron the back of the paper, the design will be transferred from the paper to the fabric (reversed). I recommend the blue lead as it both washes out and also fades out in strong sunlight.

Fine point water erasable pens

These pens are completely water erasable, their fine points make them ideal for fine work.

Trace or free hand your design directly onto the fabric using a light box.

Introduction

Transferring of the design

I have given two methods of transferring the design, graphed and freestyle.

The graphed method is transferred by laying plastic canvas (14 inch) on top of the fabric. Follow the graph, marking the fabric with a fine point water erasable pen. This method of designing is a good way to familiarise yourself with new stitches. It is also an opportunity to use canvas stitches that normally are not used on close weave linens and cottons. Decorative embroidery stitches for crazy quilt are also made easier by using the plastic canvas.

The freestyle design is transferred by tracing the design onto tracing paper with a heat transfer pencil, invert the paper onto the fabric and iron the design onto the fabric. Graphite paper or a light box may be more suitable for some fabrics.

Some designs have been reduced to fit the page, therefore, it may be necessary to **enlarge** them using a photo-copier to suit your needs.

Padded Stitches

Stitching over a padding gives the work a three dimensional look. Padding applied to open weave fabrics also gives an edge for stitches such as satin stitch to work to.

Candlewicking thread being soft and slightly fluffy helps with the coverage of satin stitch, as washing tends to bind the threads together.

Applique padding onto blankets, pullovers etc. also helps with placement, as one is able to move the pieces around until satisfied with the design before fastening down.

Colour

The muted blush of Coloured Candlewicking Cottons are perfect to keep the character of candlewicking and white work.

To create a variegated look one strand of Madeira 6 strand cotton worked in with the candlewicking thread will variegate the colour as it twists in working. A list of suggested 6 strand colours can be found on page 4.

The pale duck egg blue colour can be used by itself to create MADEIRA WORK, a form of embroidery in the 1800's deriving its name from the isle of Madeira. Pure cotton accepts dyes very well, try dyeing your favourite colours using silk or vegetable dyes. (I have found that a few metres of thread submerged in half a cup of water based silk dye and brought to the boil in the microwave works well.)

For variations of ecru use the same principle as the silk dyes using varying amounts of tea or coffee.

Candlewicking

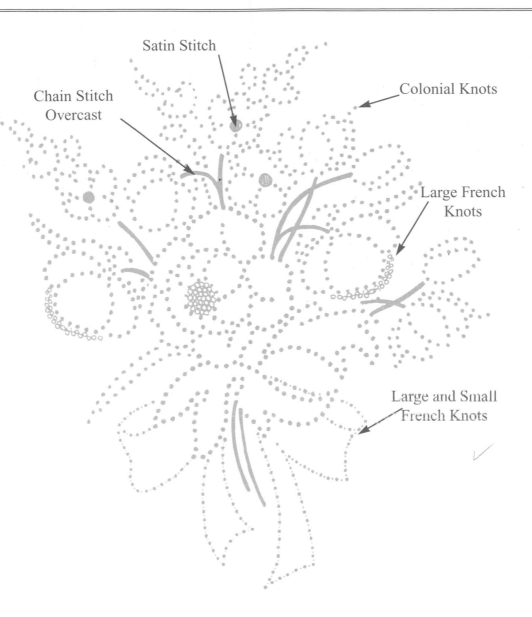

Satin Stitch

Chain Stitch
Overcast

Colonial Knots

Large French
Knots

Large and Small
French Knots

Blending colours, - Candlewicking & Madeira six strand cotton.

As described on page 3

Candlewicking Colours	*Madeira six Strand Art No 017*
Pink Blush	0403 -0404 -0405 -0606 -0605 -0303 -2309
Mauve Blush	0806 -0809 -0709 -0711 -0802 -0706 -1807
Yellow Ochre	0307 -0108 -2208 -2209 -2012 -1013 -1610
Green Blush	1511 -1512 -1513 -1310 -1603 -1604 -1209
Duck Egg Blue	1003 -1004 -1013 -1012 -1710 -1711 -1707

Work one strand each of candlewicking & six strand
together in the needle

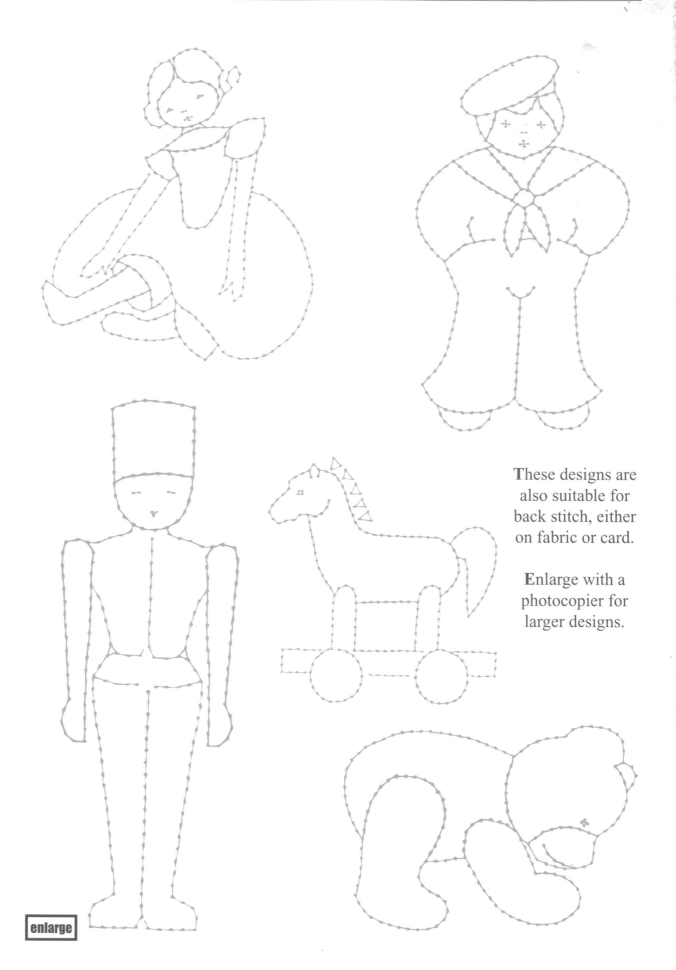

These designs are also suitable for back stitch, either on fabric or card.

Enlarge with a photocopier for larger designs.

enlarge

enlarge

Floral Candlewicking

Flower centres worked in straight stitch, bullion stitch, french knots.

enlarge

Floral Candlewicking

Work these florals in a Colonial Knot, either in natural or coloured thread. Decorate your bouquet with butterflies and bows. Join the designs together to form borders or fan out into a garland.

enlarge

Floral Candlewicking

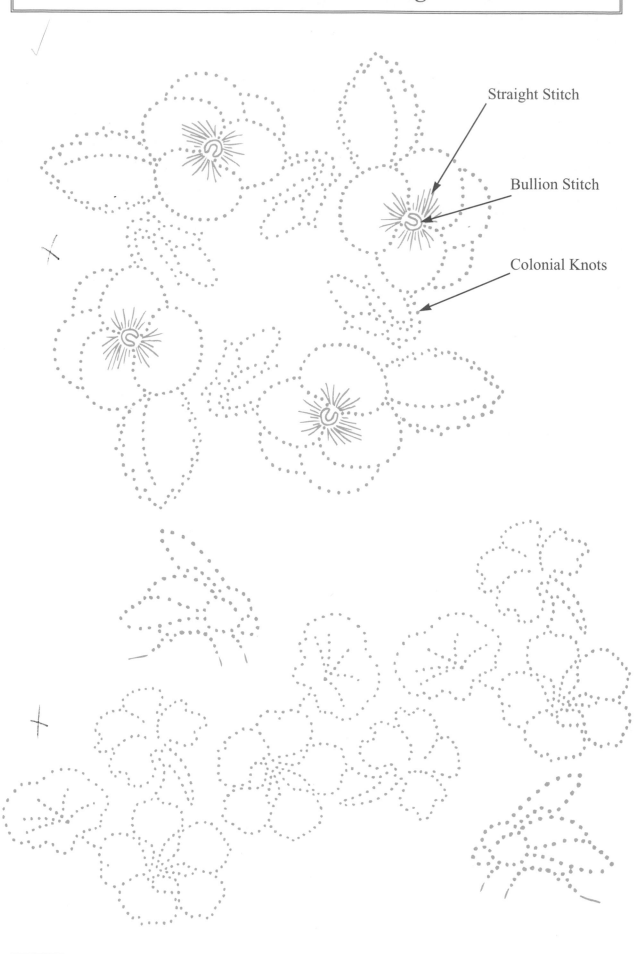

Straight Stitch

Bullion Stitch

Colonial Knots

Floral Candlewicking

Z

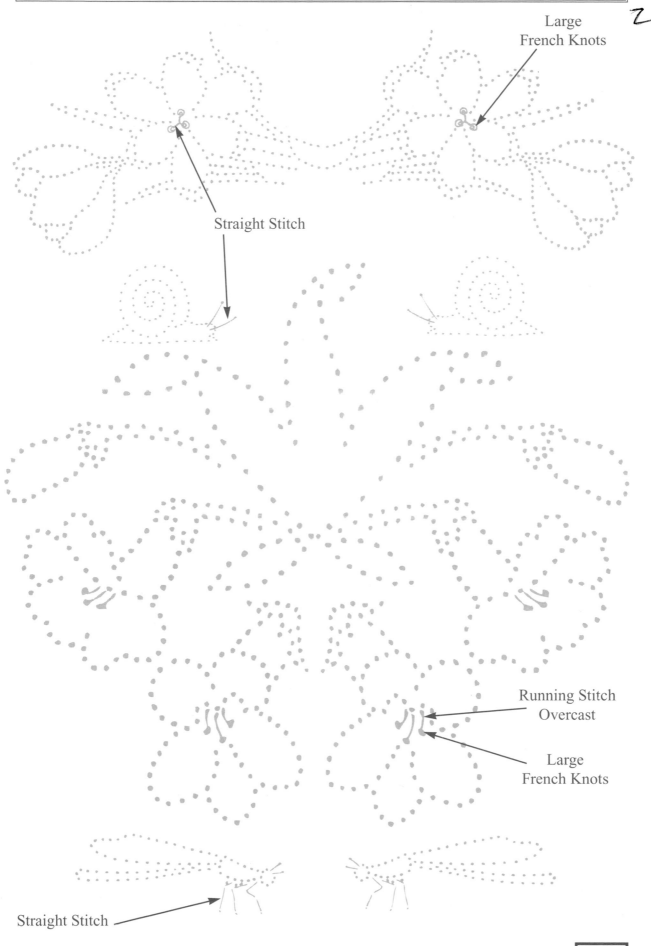

Large
French Knots

Straight Stitch

Running Stitch
Overcast

Large
French Knots

Straight Stitch

enlarge

Candlewicking Embellishments

Use these scrolled embellishments for clothing and napery. Work them in natural or coloured thread, either in heavy french knots or colonial knots These designs are also suited to beading and gold work.
Mix one strand of Madeira Glamour Art No. 9804 or Metallic Art No. 9810 to the candlewicking for sparkle. Use Glamour on its own for evening wear.

enlarge

Candlewicking Embellishments

For these designs it is important
to keep the knots close together
as in the pattern.
These designs would look
effective in simple chain stitch,
in colour, natural or Glamour.

Define the flowers
using the subtle
candlewicking colours,
green leaves and
scrolling, pink yellow or
mauve flowers.

enlarge

12

Graphed Candlewicking

Method

- Stretch and pin a 25cm sq of calico to a pin board eg Canite.

- Pin on top of the calico a panel of (14 inch) plastic canvas.

- Using a fine tipped water soluble pen, transfer the design from the graph, through the grid of the plastic canvas.

- A large hoop is recommended to maintain consistent tension.

French Knot Bullion Stitch

Lazy Daisy French Knot Straight Stitch

Graphed Candlewicking

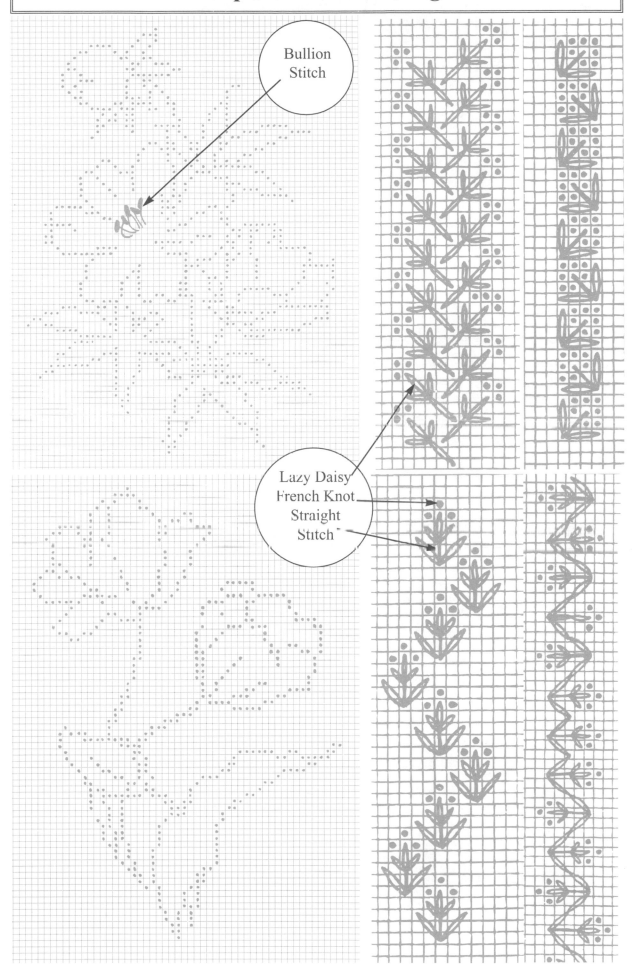

Bullion Stitch

Lazy Daisy
French Knot
Straight Stitch

Graphed Candlewicking

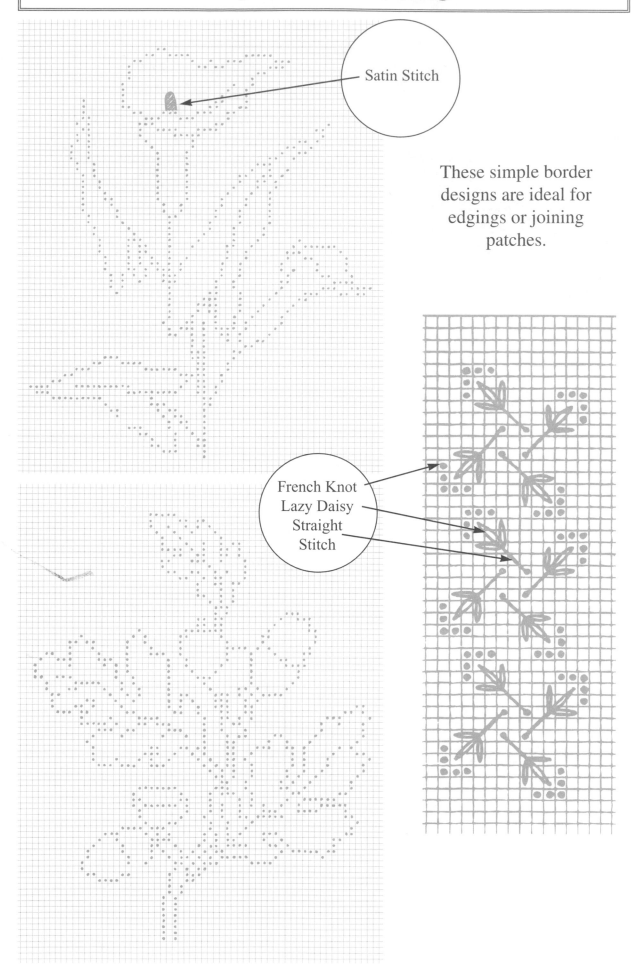

Satin Stitch

These simple border designs are ideal for edgings or joining patches.

French Knot
Lazy Daisy
Straight
Stitch

15

Canvas Style Embroidery

Method

- Stretch and pin a 25cm sq of calico to a pin board eg Canite.
- Pin on top of the calico a panel of plastic canvas *(14 inch)
- Using a fine tipped water soluble pen, transfer the design from the graph, through the grid of the plastic canvas.
- A large hoop is recommended to maintain consistent tension.

French Knot
Bullion

Lazy Daisy
Running Stitch
Overcast

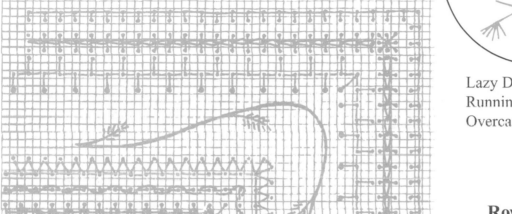

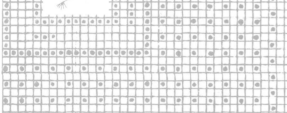

French Knots ○

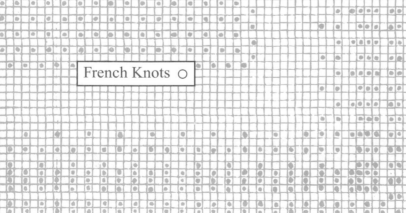

Rows from middle

1 Cross and Straight Stitch
2 Split Stitch

3 Herringbone

4 Chain Stitch

5 Straight Cross and Pin Wheel

6 Running Stitch Overcast

7 Closed Blanket Stitch

8 Straight Stitch

9 Straight Stitch and Chain

10 Straight Stitch

Quilting And Candlewicking

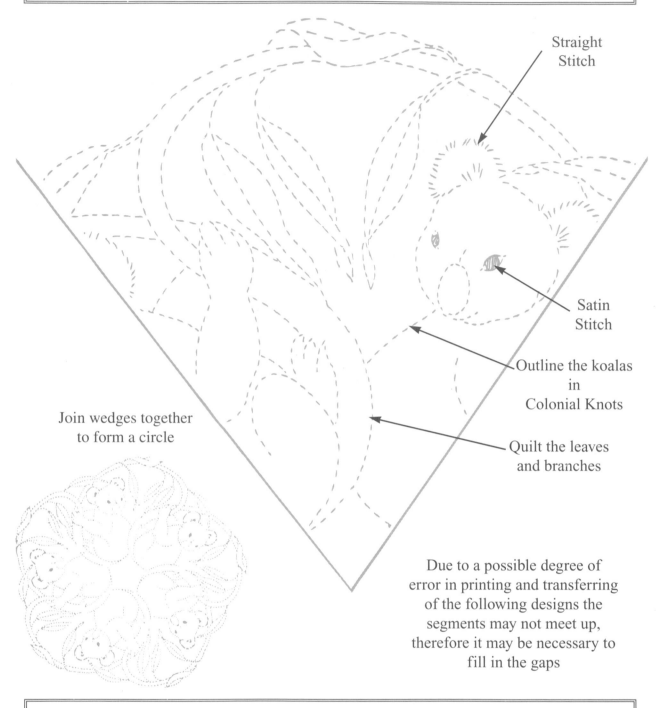

Straight
Stitch

Satin
Stitch

Outline the koalas
in
Colonial Knots

Quilt the leaves
and branches

Join wedges together
to form a circle

Due to a possible degree of
error in printing and transferring
of the following designs the
segments may not meet up,
therefore it may be necessary to
fill in the gaps

Petite Knots

These petite designs are for tiny knots, worked
close together.
Use a single strand of candlewicking thread or
two to three strands of stranded cotton. Single
turn french knots create a subtle design, for
greater contrast vary the turns of the knot.

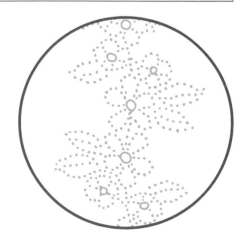

enlarge

Quilting And Candlewicking

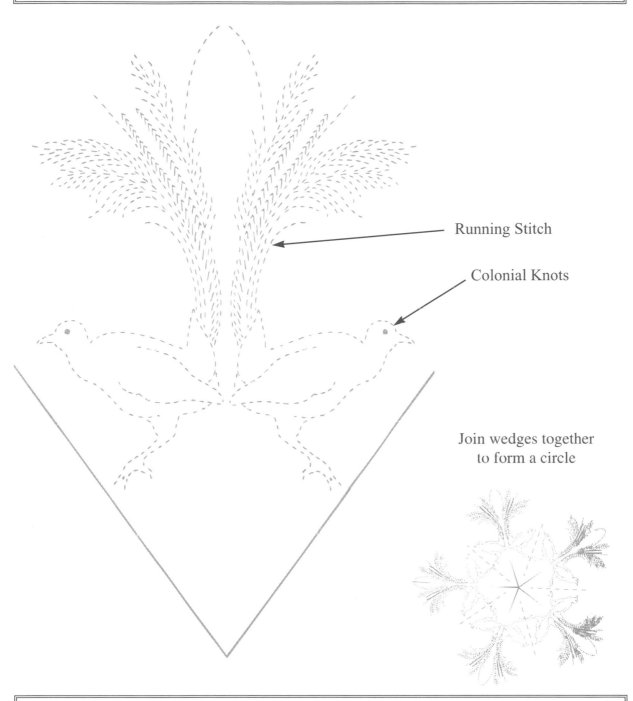

Running Stitch

Colonial Knots

Join wedges together
to form a circle

Petite Knots

enlarge

Quilting And Candlewicking

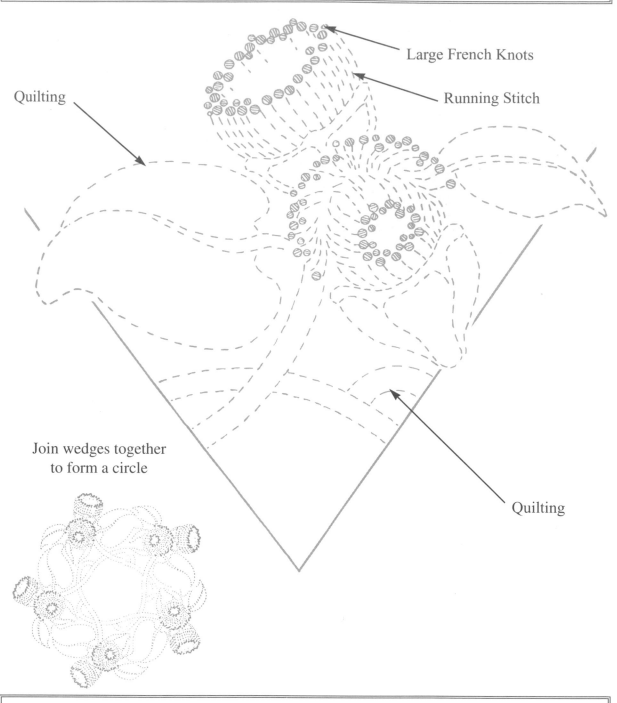

Large French Knots

Running Stitch

Quilting

Join wedges together
to form a circle

Quilting

Petite Knots

enlarge

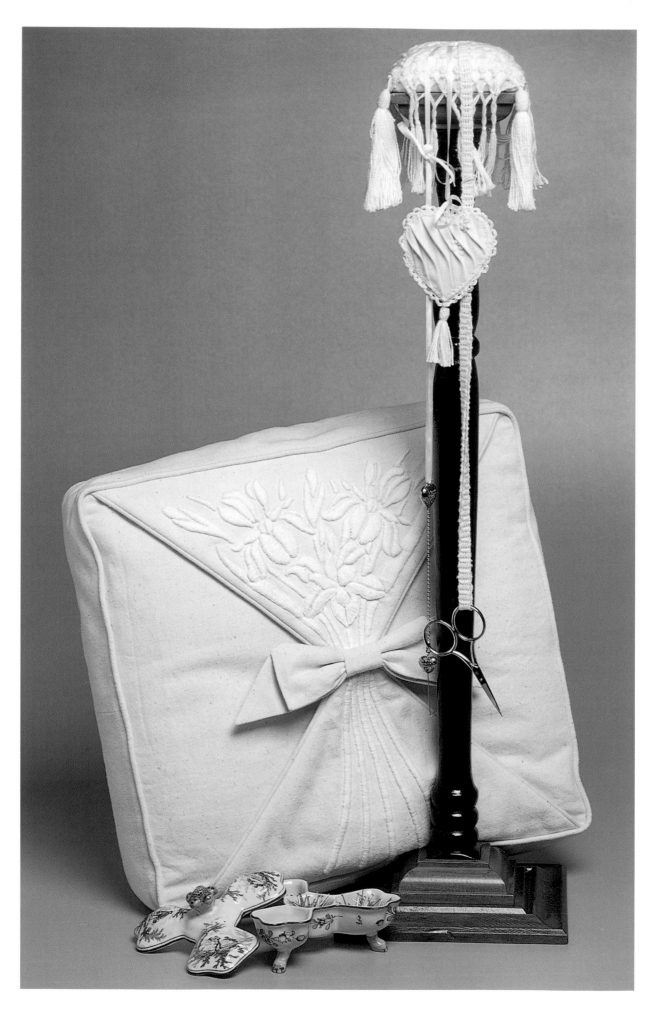

Quilting And Candlewicking

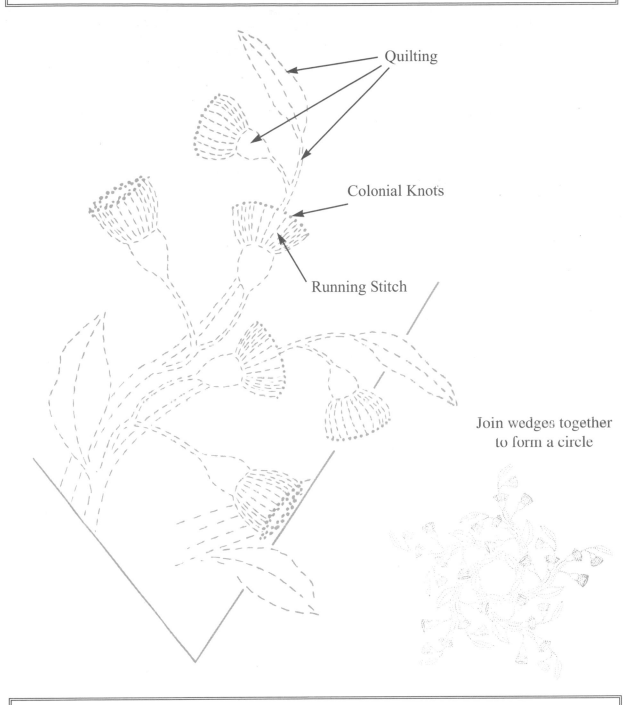

Quilting

Colonial Knots

Running Stitch

Join wedges together
to form a circle

Petite Knots

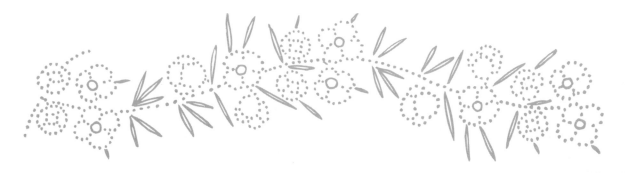

enlarge

Quilting And Candlewicking

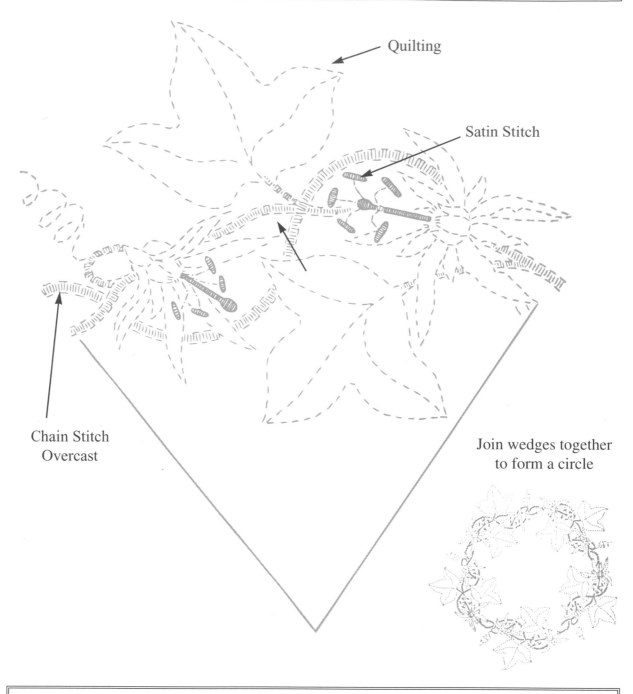

Quilting

Satin Stitch

Chain Stitch
Overcast

Join wedges together
to form a circle

Petite Knots

enlarge

Quilting And Candlewicking

Quilted leaves and branches
Colonial Knot flowers

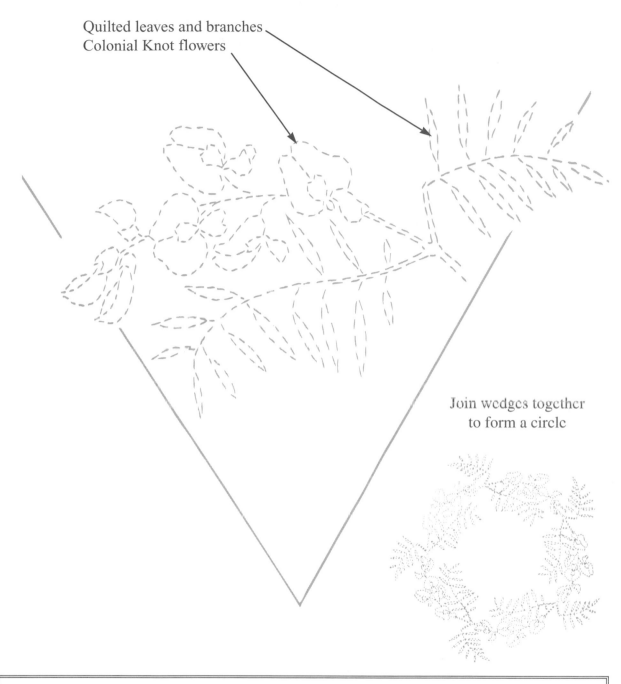

Join wedges together
to form a circle

Petite Knots

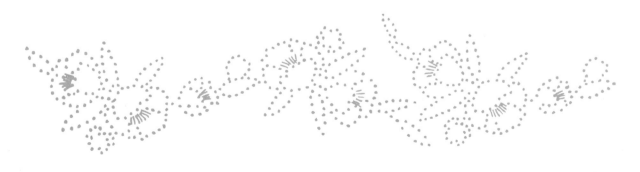

enlarge

White Work

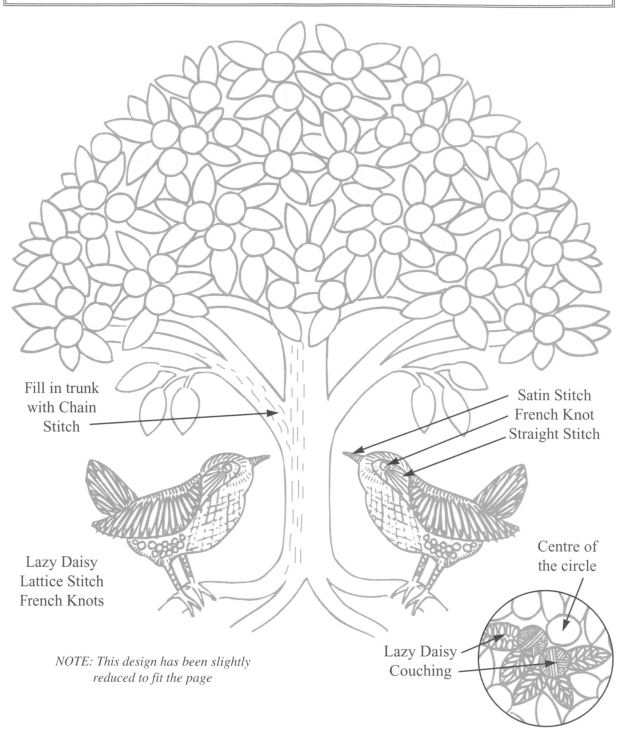

Fill in trunk
with Chain
Stitch

Satin Stitch
French Knot
Straight Stitch

Lazy Daisy
Lattice Stitch
French Knots

Centre of
the circle

Lazy Daisy
Couching

*NOTE: This design has been slightly
reduced to fit the page*

This particular design, although giving the illusion of being a difficult piece, has only simple stitches, lazy daisy, running stitch overcast, chain stitch, straight stitch; french knots, and satin stitch.

The padded fruit are created by using 7mm pom poms *(available through craft stores)*

- Thread a pom pom onto a length of thread.
- Pass the needle down through the centre of a circle, drawing the pom pom firmly to the fabric.
- Couch over the pom pom moving around the circle, the threads criss crossing over the centre of the pom pom.

enlarge

White Work

Rabbits

- **Lazy Daisy**
  for all the leaves
- **Chain Stitch**
  for the thicker branches
- **Lattice Stitch**
  for filling in the body
- **French Knot**
  for nose, tail and eye
- **Running Stitch overcast**
  for the outline of the body

Liliums

- **Chain Stitch**
  for ribbon
- **Satin Stitch**
  for flowers, buds, leaves, stems
- **Bullion Stitch**
  for the stamen

Birds

- **Chain Stitch**
  for square border and circular bough
- **Lazy Daisy**
  for leaves
- **Running stitch overcast**
  for the body of the birds
- **French Knot**
  for the eyes

To create the full design, divide the fabric into quarters. *(with a tacking stitch or with a removable pencil mark)* Transfer the design into each quarter.

Due to a possible degree of error in printing and transferring of the design the quarters may not meet up, therefore it may be necessary to fill in the gaps

enlarge

Posies

- **Lazy Daisy**
  for leaves
- **Satin Stitch**
  for bow
- **Blanket Stitch**
  for flowers
- **French Knots**
  for the centres
- **Couching**
  for flower stems

Vines

- **Couched Chain**
  for main vine branch
- **Running Stitch Overcast**
  for leaf stems
- **Lazy Daisy**
  for the leaves

Elephants

- **Running Stitch Overcast**
  for the outline of the elephants
- **Satin Stitch**
  for the grass and palm trunks
- **Lazy Daisy**
  for the palm leaves
- **Padded Satin**
  for palm nuts
- **Beads and assorted stitches**
  eg Button hole, Bullion,
  French Knot, Lazy Daisy for
  the blanket

enlarge

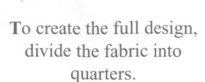

To create the full design, divide the fabric into quarters.
(with a tacking stitch or with a removable pencil mark)
Transfer the design into each quarter.

Due to a possible degree of error in printing and transferring of the design the quarters may not meet up, therefore it may be necessary to fill in the gaps

The sizes of these designs are suitable for cushions and mirror borders. With a change of size they might be used for clothing, bags, manchester, and much more.

enlarge

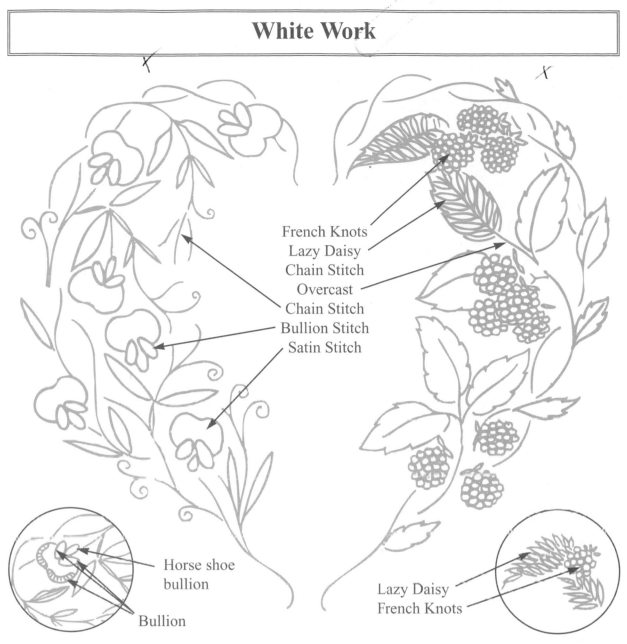

French Knots
Lazy Daisy
Chain Stitch
Overcast
Chain Stitch
Bullion Stitch
Satin Stitch

Horse shoe bullion

Bullion

Lazy Daisy
French Knots

Sweet Pea

The sweet pea flower is formed by working satin stitch over two bullion stitches placed at the top of each flower. The satin stitch is fanned out from the centre, to the outer edge.

Three bullions are then worked over the bottom of the fan.

(the middle bullion is a horse shoe bullion)

Berry Fruit

The berries are formed with French knots of differing sizes. Three to four, six turn double thread knots in the centre of each berry. Ten turn single thread knots around the outer edge. To create greater texture work background berries with six turn single thread knots.

Transferring the design

Trace the chosen side on to tracing paper with a blue heat transfer pencil.
Transfer the design onto the fabric. *(following transfer pencil instructions)*
With the transfer pencil, repeat the design on the reverse side of the tracing paper.
Match the tracing with the other half of the heart.

enlarge

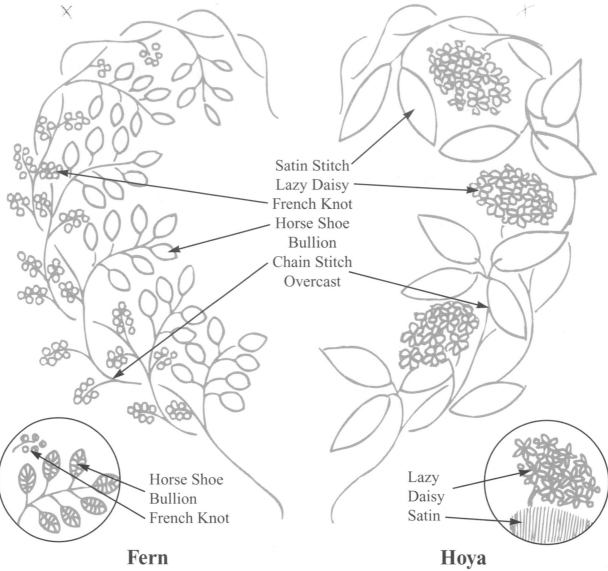

Satin Stitch
Lazy Daisy
French Knot
Horse Shoe
Bullion
Chain Stitch
Overcast

Horse Shoe
Bullion
French Knot

Lazy
Daisy
Satin

Fern

Fern leaves are worked in horse shoe bullion and four turn single thread French knots. Branches are worked in chain stitch overcast.

Hoya

The hoya flowers are worked in lazy daisy, the leaves in satin stitch. Branches are worked in chain stitch overcast.

Stitches from the Heart

The line work is all stitched in running stitch overcast, the dots at the end of the lines created with French knots.

enlarge

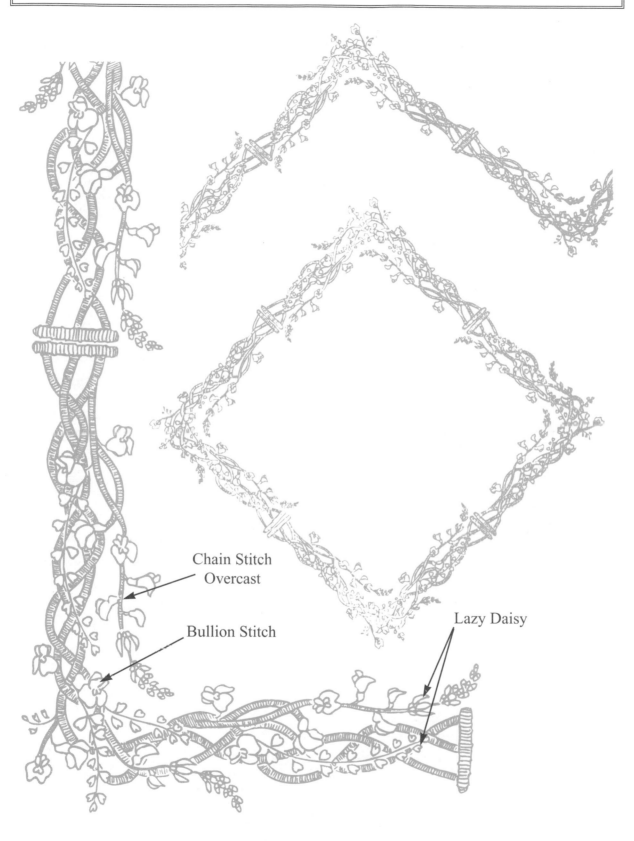

Chain Stitch
Overcast

Bullion Stitch

Lazy Daisy

Change the shape of the vines
depending on the way they are placed,
zig zag or square

enlarge

White Work

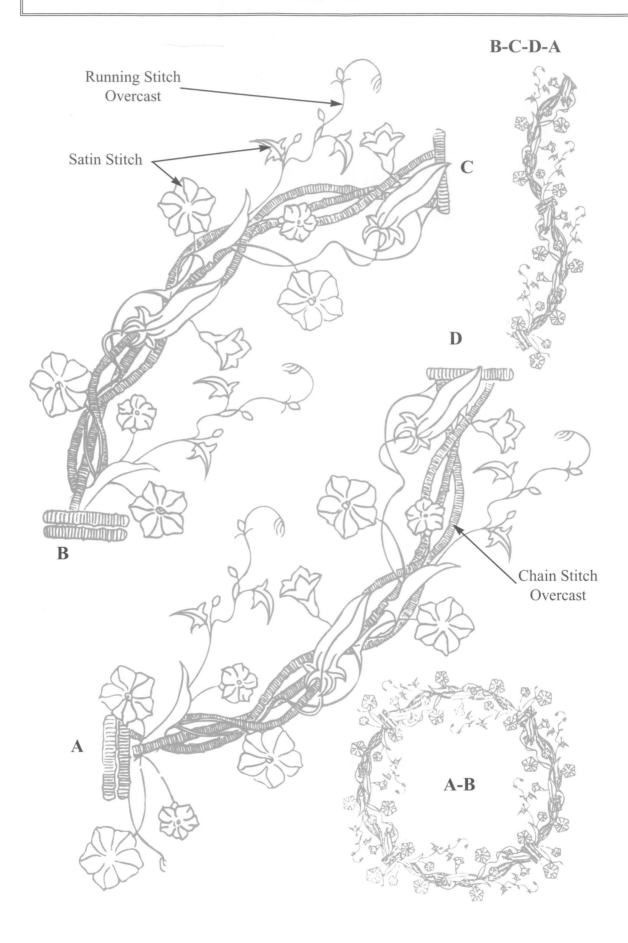

Running Stitch Overcast

Satin Stitch

B-C-D-A

C

D

B

Chain Stitch Overcast

A

A-B

enlarge

Lazy Daisy
French Knots
Delica Beads 211
Horse Shoe Bullion
Bullion Stitch
Running Stitch
Overcast

Bouquet
Work in Lazy Daisy, French Knot, Bullion and Straight Stitch

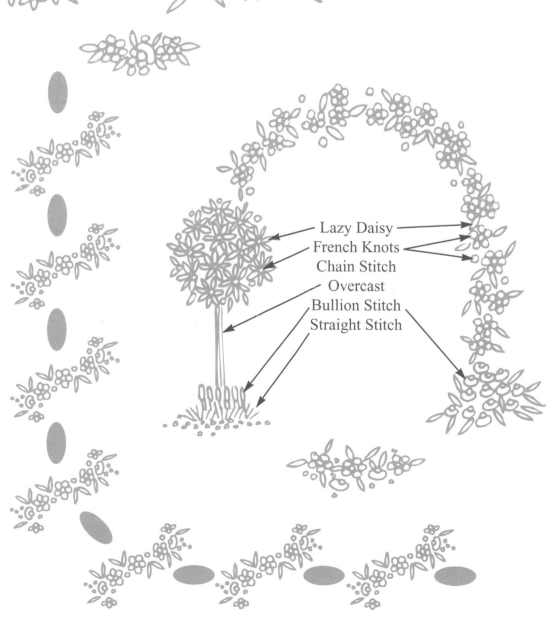

Lazy Daisy
French Knots
Chain Stitch
Overcast
Bullion Stitch
Straight Stitch

Ribbon Border

White Work

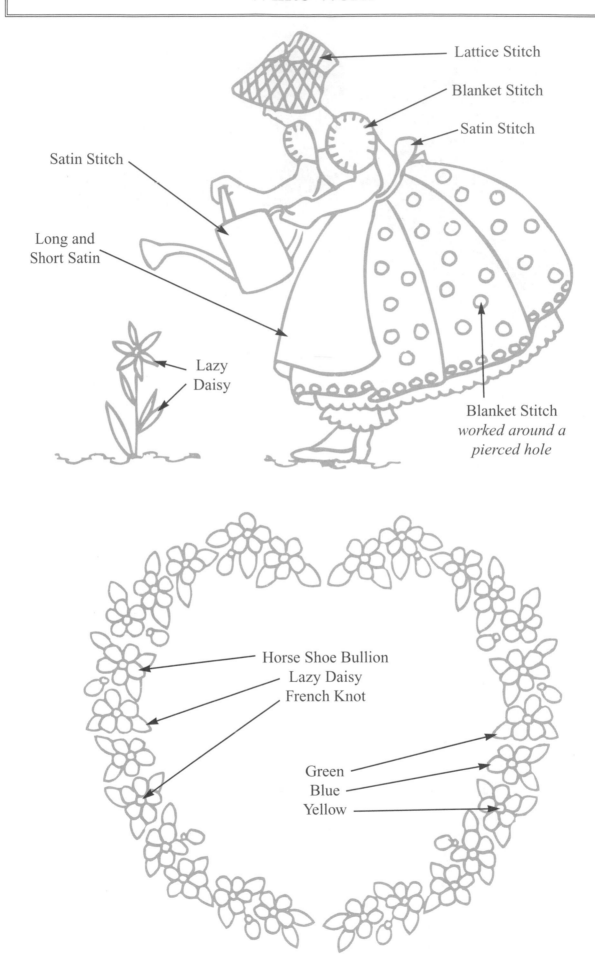

Lattice Stitch

Blanket Stitch

Satin Stitch

Satin Stitch

Long and
Short Satin

Lazy
Daisy

Blanket Stitch
*worked around a
pierced hole*

Horse Shoe Bullion
Lazy Daisy
French Knot

Green
Blue
Yellow

Padded Embroidery

Padded Irises

The worked model of this design is candlewicking thread on linen. The complete design has been padded with synthetic felt. This raises the profile of the design. Padding also makes satin stitch and extended lazy daisy easier.

Method:

- Choose a felt either the colour of the background fabric or the colour of the thread.
- Apply fusible webbing to one side of the felt.
  (Use VLElSOFlX paper backed fusible webbing.)
- Trace the design on to the shiny side of the backing paper with a soft lead pencil.
- Place the shiny side on to the glue side of the felt and iron
- The design is now printed on to the felt.
- Cut out the pieces, arrange, and iron into place.

Blanket Stitch
Satin Stitch

Note
The sizes of designs have been changed to fit the page

Work Cushion
This design has been made up into a work cushion.
See next page

enlarge

42

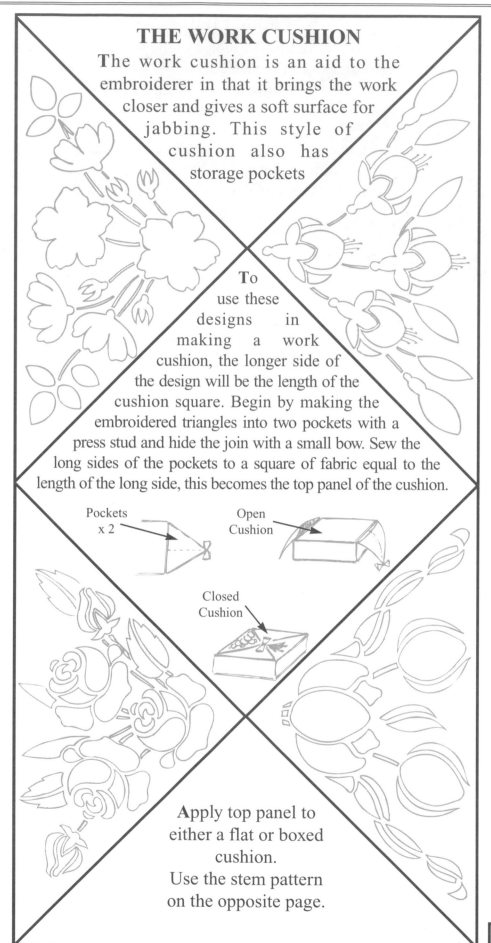

Padded Embroidery

THE WORK CUSHION

The work cushion is an aid to the embroiderer in that it brings the work closer and gives a soft surface for jabbing. This style of cushion also has storage pockets

To use these designs in making a work cushion, the longer side of the design will be the length of the cushion square. Begin by making the embroidered triangles into two pockets with a press stud and hide the join with a small bow. Sew the long sides of the pockets to a square of fabric equal to the length of the long side, this becomes the top panel of the cushion.

Pockets x 2

Open Cushion

Closed Cushion

Apply top panel to either a flat or boxed cushion.
Use the stem pattern on the opposite page.

enlarge

Padded Embroidery

Use a mixture of single and double threads. A single strand of 6 strand embroidery cotton can be added to variegate the colour.

THE BASIC TASSEL

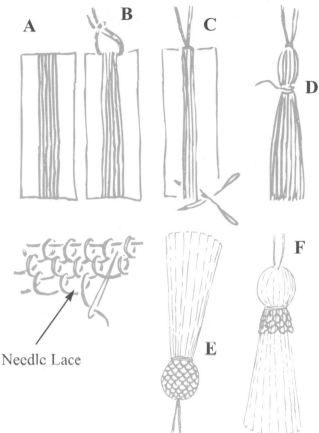

- Cut a piece of strong card the length of the tassel required.
- Wrap the card with tassel thread as in fig A.
- Secure with strong cord as in fig B.
- Cut tassel thread as in fig C.
- Fasten with a matching or contrasting thread, if needle lace is to be added leave a 30cm tail as in fig D.

Needle Lace

ADDING NEEDLE LACE

- Fig E invert the tassel and work the lace stitch towards the cord, it may be necessary to cast off towards the end.
- Fig F work the lace stitch towards the cut end of the tassel.
- Decorate with beads or embroider lacework. Join several tassels together to form a large tassel.

BLANKET STITCH TASSEL

- Wrap strong card with tassel thread as in fig A.
- Blanket stitch over the tassel thread as in fig G and H.
- Remove card, join and cut as in fig I or J.
- Join several together to form a large tassel as in fig K.

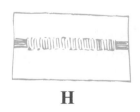

POM-POM TASSEL

- **M**ake a conventional pom-pom, filling the centre hole to just over ⅔. *Do NOT cut away from the card.*
- **M**ake a basic tassel to the stage of fig C, make it a little larger than the ⅓ hole left in the pom-pom.
- **J**oin the pom-pom and the tassel together as fig L.
- **C**ut the thread on the pom-pom.
- **S**ecure both tassel and pom-pom with a binding thread in finishing off the pom-pom.

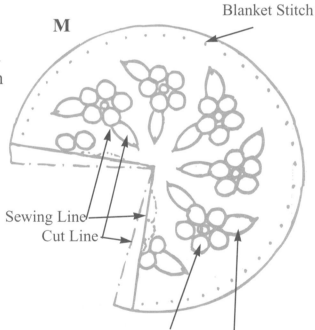

L

Pom
Pom
Tassel
Winding
Thread

CONE TASSEL

- **M**ark and cut out circle of fabric as fig M.
- **E**mbroider, blanket stitch the edges, and sew together to make a cone.
- **M**ake a large, basic tassel and six smaller tassels.
- **T**hread the cord of the large tassel through the point of the cone from the inside.
- **S**ew the smaller tassel at even intervals around the edge of the fabric.
- **T**his form of tassel is particularly good when the tassel needs to match fabric on cushions etc.

M

Blanket Stitch

Sewing Line
Cut Line

French Knot   Lazy Daisy

THREADS SUITABLE FOR TASSELS

- Candlewicking thread, Madeira Stranded Cotton, Stranded Silk, Decora Rayon, Glamour, Decor, Metallic No 3, No 5, No 8, No 10.

Stitch Glossary

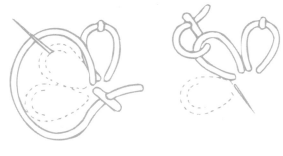

Lazy Daisy

French Knot

Blanket Stitch

Straight Stitch

Satin Stitch

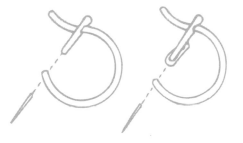

Split Stitch

Colonial Knot (left hand)

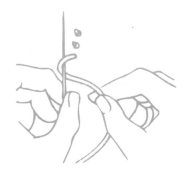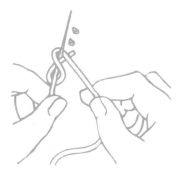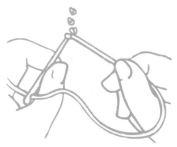

48

Stitch Glossary

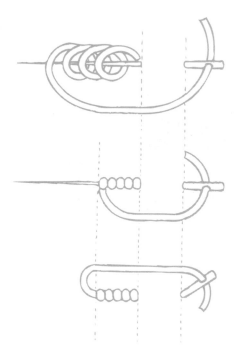

Pin Wheel

Closed Buttonhole

Bullion Stitch

Lattice Stitch

Running Stitch

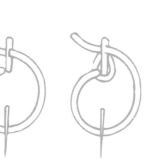

Chain Stitch

Running Stitch
Overcast

Colonial Knot (right hand)

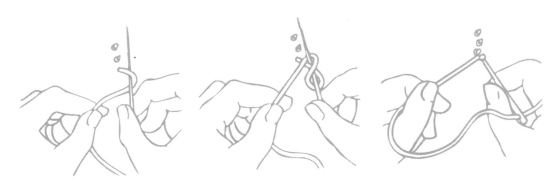

Monograms

Satin Stitch

Candlewicking

French Knots
&
Lazy Daisy

Monograms and whitework are traditional partners, these letters have been chosen for their sturdiness, which makes them ideal for satin stitch.

Satin stitch is easier if the outline is firstly worked in running stitch or bullion stitch if a padded look is desired.

Satin Stitch
Lazy Daisy
French Knot

Lazy Daisy
Bullion Stitch
Running Stitch
Overcast

Christmas
1997

Christmas

Christmas
White work and Christmas go so well together, work these designs
for the festive season.

Sources & Suppliers

Published by Aussie Publishers 25 Izett Street, Prahran 3181

Tel: +61-3-9529 4400 **Fax:** +61-3-9525 1172
Email: penguin@netspace.net.au **Website:** http://www.penguin-threads.com.au

Other books and videos distributed by AUSSIE Publishers

Books **Gary Clarke**
- Embroidery and Candlewicking Designs
- Cats: Inspiration for Needlework
- Bouquets, Bows and Bugs
- Simply Flowers

Leisa Pownall
- Beautiful Bullions

Pamela Gurney
- Punch Crazy

Stewart Merrett
- Appliqué Art
- Appliqué Alphabet
- Cross Stitch Pack

Tony Barber
- Toy Book

Jenny Haskins
- Amadeus
- Machine Embroidery, Inspirational Quilting Techniques

Judy Thomson
- Heirloom Timepiece

Anne van der Kley
- Serging Australia

Videos **Jenny Haskins**
- A Touch of Class – Sewing with Metallic Threads
- Over the Top – Decorative Overlocking/Serging

Leisa Pownall
- The A to Z of Hand Embroidery
- More Embroidery Stitches and Shadow Embroidery
- Animals & Flowers in Bullion Stitch
- The Wonderful World of Smocking

Eileen Campbell
- Machine Appliqué
- Basic Free Machine Embroidery
- An Introduction to Machine Quilting

Nola Fossey
- Creating Wearable Art

Gabriella Verstraeten
- Having Fun with Machine Embroidery
- Appliqué with a Difference

Tony Barber
- Toy Book Video

USA DISTRIBUTOR

QUILTER'S RESOURCE INC.

2211 North Elston Avenue
Chicago, Illinois 60614 USA
Tel: +1-773-278 5695
Fax: +1-773-278 1348

Notes